Q

QUAIL

First published in Great Britain in 2012 by
Quail Publishing
www.quailpublishing.co.uk

An imprint of Daco Technology Ltd

Copyright © Quail Publishing 2012

Designs: Sarah Hatton
Photography: Moy Williams
Styling: Sarah Hatton
Hair & Makeup: Nadia Altinbas
Graphic Design: Darren Brant

ISBN 978-0-9567851-2-1

Printed in the United Kingdom

Introduction

Welcome to my second book of simple knits to keep you and your loved ones warm and cosy. I have designed this book to encourage as many people into the world of hand knitting as possible.

I learnt to knit as a child and have always been passionate about fashion. After gaining my degree I was lucky enough to enter the world of handknit, professionally. I have been in the industry for over 10 years and have worked for brands including Rowan, Patons, Sirdar and Sublime. I love the hands-on approach that hand knit offers, it's also wonderful to be able to make gifts for loved ones as well as stylish garments for yourself.

I have taken my favourite winter yarns from the Rowan range and designed 10 simple projects. For each project you will find a list of equipment, how much yarn you will need and a clear, simple set of instructions free from the usual knitting jargon that can be terrifying for
the beginner! Each pattern helps you learn a brand new technique, so before you know it you will have mastered knitting!

I have also produced some instructional videos as part of my knitting App available from the iTunes App Store. I hope you enjoy making the projects and don't forget to keep in touch via my website; www.sarahhatton.com

Drover Wristwarmers

10 More Simple Cosy Projects

Homely Cowl

Homely Cowl

10 More Simple Cosy Projects

Pioneer Cape

Buccaneer Hat

Buccaneer Hat

10 More Simple Cosy Projects

Sylvan Jumper & Wanderer Cardigan

10 More Simple Cosy Projects

Ranch Legwarmers

10 More Simple Cosy Projects

Outland Scarf

10 More Simple Cosy Projects

Voyager Hat

Wanderer Cardigan

10 More Simple Cosy Projects

10 More Simple Cosy Projects

Venturer Tunic

Buccaneer hat
pg. 30

Sylvan jumper
pg. 32

Voyager hat
pg. 37

Wanderer cardigan
pg. 38

Venturer tunic
pg. 42

— Drover Wristwarmers —

Materials:

YARN USED

Rowan Kid Classic

1 x 50gm (shown in Victoria 852)

NEEDLES

1 pair 5mm (US 8) needles.

Cable needle

WRISTWARMERS (make 2 alike)

Cast on 36 stitches.

Row 1 (right side): Purl 2, * knit 4, purl 3, repeat from * to last 6 stitches, knit 4, purl 2.

Row 2: Knit 2, purl 4, * knit 3, purl 4, repeat from * to last 2 stitches, knit 2.

Rows 3 and 4: As row 1 and 2.

Row 5: Purl 2, * slip next 2 stitches onto a cable needle and leave at back of work, knit 2, then knit 2 from cable needle, purl 3, repeat from * to last 6 stitches, slip next 2 stitches onto a cable needle and leave at back of work, knit 2, then knit 2 from cable needle, purl 2.

Row 6: Knit 2, purl 4, * knit 3, purl 4, repeat from * to last 2 stitches, knit 2.

These 6 rows set pattern.

Continue in pattern until work measures approx. 21cm/8¼in or length required, ending with row 2 of pattern.

Cast off in pattern.

Using mattress stitch, join seam for approx. 4cm/1½in (this will form the part that wraps around your hand), leave a gap of approx. 4cm/1½in (this will form the hole for your thumb) then join remainder of seam.

Homely Cowl

Materials:

YARN USED

Rowan Big Wool

3 x 100gm (shown in Oxidised 059)

Each ball will work approx.
52cm/20½in of scarf.

NEEDLES

1 pair 12mm (US 1) needles.

Cast on 22 stitches.

Row 1: Knit.

Row 2: Knit 2, purl 18, knit 2.

These 2 rows set pattern.

Continue in pattern as set until work
measures 180cm/71in, ending with
right side facing for next row.

Cast off.

MAKING UP

Join cast on and cast off edges to
form a loop.

Pioneer Cape

TO FIT

S	M	L	XL	XXL	
81~86	92~97	101~107	112~117	122~127	cm
32~34	36~38	40~42	44~46	48~50	in

Actual Measurements (laid flat)

Width at hem 56 [61:69:76:81]cm/22 [24:27:30:32]in

Length 31 [33:35:37:39]cm/12 [13:14:14½:15½]in

MATERIALS

YARN USED

Rowan Big Wool 3 [3:4:4:5] x 100gm

(shown in Glum 056)

NEEDLES

1 pair 12mm (US 1) needles.

TENSION

8 stitches and 12 rows to 10cm/4in measured over stocking stitch on 12mm needles.

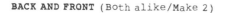

BACK AND FRONT (Both alike/Make 2)

Cast on 45 [49:55:61:67] stitches.

Knit 4 rows.

Continue in stocking stitch (1 row knit, 1 row purl) until work measures 18 [20:22:24:26] cm/7 [8:8½:9½:10] in, ending with right side facing for next row.

Next row: Knit 1, slip 1, knit 1, pass slipped stitch over, knit to last 3 stitches, knit 2 together, knit 1. (43 [47:53:59:65] stitches remain).

Beginning with a purl row, work 3 rows in stocking stitch.

Next row: Knit 1, slip 1, knit 1, pass slipped stitch over, knit to last 3 stitches, knit 2 together, knit 1. (41 [45:51:57:63] stitches remain).

Purl 1 row.

Repeat the last 2 rows twice more.
(37 [41:47:53:59] stitches).

Cast off 2 [3:4:5:6] stitches at beg
of next 4 rows. (29 [29:31:33:35]
stitches remain).

Cast off 3 [2:3:4:4] stitches at beg
of next 2 rows. (23 [25:25:25:27]
stitches remain).

Work 4 rows more in stocking stitch.

Knit 3 rows, ending with wrong side
facing for next row.

Cast off knitways on wrong side.

MAKING UP

Join side seams.

Buccaneer Hat

Materials:

YARN USED

Rowan Cocoon (shown in Shale 804)

1 x 50gm

Plus oddments of other yarn for pompon

NEEDLES

1 pair 6mm (US 10) needles.

1 pair 7mm (US 10½) needles.

Using 6mm needles cast on 73 stitches.

Row 1: Knit 1, * purl 1, knit 1, repeat from * to end.

Row 2: * Purl 1, knit 1, repeat from * to last stitch, purl 1.

These 2 rows set rib.

Work a further 6 rows in rib.

Change to 7mm needles.

Rows 1 to 4: Knit.

Row 5: Knit.

Row 6: Purl.

Row 7: Knit.

Row 8: Purl.

These 8 rows set pattern.

Continue in pattern repeating from Row 1~8 until work measures 18cm/7in, ending with right side facing for next row.

Shape crown

Next row: (Knit 7, knit 2 together) 8 times, knit 1.(65 stitches remain)

Pattern 1 row.

Next row: (Knit 6, knit 2 together) 8 times, knit 1. (57 stitches remain)

Pattern 1 row.

Next row: (Knit 5, knit 2 together) 8 times, knit 1. (49 stitches remain)

Pattern 1 row.

Next row: (Knit 4, knit 2 together) 8 times, knit 2. (41 stitches remain)

Pattern 1 row.

Next row: (Knit 3, knit 2 together) 8 times, knit 1.(33 stitches remain)

Pattern 1 row.

Next row: (Knit 2, knit 2 together)
8 times, knit 1. (25 stitches remain)

Next row: Pattern 1, (pattern
2 together) 12 times.
(13 stitches remain)

Next row: (Knit 2 together) 6 times,
knit 1. (7 stitches)

Break off yarn and thread through
the remaining stitches and pull
together.

Fasten off.

MAKING UP

Using mattress stitch join back
seam.

Using the remaining yarn along with
oddments of other yarn make a pompon
approx. 8cm/3in diameter and attach
to top of hat.

Sylvan Jumper

TO FIT

S	M	L	XL	XXL	
81~86	92~97	101~107	112~117	122~127	cm
32~34	36~38	40~42	44~46	48~50	in

Actual Measurements (laid flat)

Width   44 [49:55:61:68]cm/17¼ [19¼:21½:24:27]in

Length 52 [54:56:58:60]cm/20½ [21½:22:23:23½]in

Sleeve length:

29 [29:30:30:31]cm/11½ [11½:12:12:12¼]in
(after turnback)

MATERIALS

YARN USED

Rowan Lima (shown in Andes 880)

8 [9:10:10:11] x 50gm

NEEDLES

1 pair 5½mm (US 9) needles

1 pair 4½mm (US 7) needles

TENSION

20 stitches and 26 rows to 10cm/4in
measured over stocking stitch on
5½mm (US 9) needles.

....

BACK and FRONT (both alike)
Using 4½mm needles cast on
88 [98:110:122:136] stitches.

Work in garter stitch (every
row knit) until work measures 6
[6:7:7:7]cm/2½ [2½:2¾:2¾2¾]in,
ending with right side facing for
next row.

Change to 5½mm needles and beginning
with a knit row, continue in stocking
stitch (1 row knit, 1 row purl) until
work measures 31 [32:33:34:35]cm
/12¼ [12½:13:13½:14]in, ending with
right side facing for next row.

Shape armholes
Decrease 1 stitch at each end
of next 6 [6:8:8:10] rows.
(76 [86:94:106:116] stitches
remain)

Continue without shaping until armhole measures 12 [13:13:14:14] cm/4½ [5:5:5½:5½]in, ending with right side facing for next row.

Shape neck
Next row: Knit 23 [28:32:38:43], turn and leave remaining stitches on a holder.

Working on these stitches only continue as follows:-

Work 1 row.

Decrease 1 stitch at neck edge of next 5 rows, then on every following alternate row until 14 [19:22:28:32] stitches remain.

Cont without shaping until armhole measures 20 [21:22:23:24]cm/ 8 [8¼:8½:9:9½]in, ending with right side facing for next row.

Shape shoulder
Next row: Cast off 7 [9:11:14:16] stitches, knit to end.

Work 1 row.

Cast off remaining stitches.

With right side facing, rejoin yarn to remaining stitches, cast off centre 30 stitches, knit to end.

Work 1 row.

Decrease 1 stitch at neck edge of next 5 rows, then on every following alternate row until 14 [19:22:28:32] stitches.

Continue without shaping until armhole measures 20 [21:22:23:24] cm/8 [8¼:8½:9:9½]in, ending with wrong side facing for next row.

Shape shoulder
Next row: Cast off 7 [9:11:14:16] stitches, purl to end.

Work 1 row.
Cast off remaining stitches.

SLEEVES (Both alike)
Using 4½mm needles cast on 52 [54:56:58:60] stitches.

Work in garter stitch (every row knit) for 10 [10:12:12:12]cm/ 4 [4:4½:4½:4½]in, ending with right side facing for next row.

Change to 5½mm needles.

Beginning with a knit row and working in stocking stitch throughout, increase 1 stitch at each end of 3rd and 0 [1:2:3:4] following alternate rows and then on every following 4th row to 78 [82:86:90:94] stitches.

Continue until work measures 34 [34:36:36:37]cm/13½ [13½:14:14:14½]in, ending with right side facing for next row.

Shape sleeve top
Decrease 1 stitch at each end of next 6 [6:8:8:10] rows. (66 [70:70:74:74] stitches remain)

Cast off 10 stiches at beginning of next 6 rows. (6 [10:10:14:14] stitches remain)

Cast off remaining stitches.

MAKING UP
Join right shoulder seam, using mattress stitch.

Neckband
With right side facing, using
4½mm needles pick up and knit
18 [18:20:20:20] stitches down left
side of front neck, 30 stitches from
cast off stitches at front neck,
18 [18:20:20:20] stitches up right
side of front neck, 18 [18:20:20:20]
stitches down side of back neck,
30 stitches from cast off stitches
at back neck and 18 [18:20:20:20]
stitches up side of back neck.(132
[132:140:140:140] stitches).

Knit 1 row.

Next row: * Knit 1, knit 2 together,
knit 60 [60:64:64:64],knit 2 together,
knit 1 *, repeat from * to *.
128 [128:136:136:136] stitches
remain.

Knit 3 rows.

Next row: * Knit 1, knit 2 together,
knit 58 [58:62:62:62], knit 2 together,
knit 1 *, repeat from * to *.
124 [124:132:132:132] stitches
remain.

Knit 3 rows.

Next row: * Knit 1, knit 2 together,
knit 56 [56:60:60:60], knit 2 together,
knit 1 *, rep from * to *.
(120 [120:128:128:128] stitches
remain)

Cast off knitways.

MAKING UP
Join left shoulder and neckband seam.

Join side seams using mattress stitch.
Join sleeve seams, using mattress
stitch and reversing seam for first
half of garter stitch cuff to form
turnback cuff. Sew cuff in position if
desired. Sew in sleeves.

Ranch Legwarmers

Materials:

YARN USED

Rowan Kid Classic (shown in Bittersweet 866)

2 x 50gm

NEEDLES

1 pair 5mm (US 8) needles.

TENSION

19 stitches and 25 rows to 10cm/4in measured over stocking stitch on 5mm (US 8) needles.

Cast on 46 stitches.

Row 1 (right side): Knit 2, * purl 2, knit 2, repeat from * to end.

Row 2: * Purl 2, knit 2, repeat from * to last 2 stitches, purl 2.

These 2 rows set rib.

Work 6 rows more in rib.

Beginning with a knit row and working in stocking stitch (1 row knit, 1 row purl) throughout work 20 rows.

Decrease 1 stitch at each end of next and foll 24th row. (42 stitches remain)

Continue without shaping until work measures 36cm/9½in, ending with right side facing for next row.

Work 8 rows in rib.

Cast off in rib. Using mattress stitch join back seam.

Outland Scarf

Materials:

YARN USED

Rowan Big Wool

Shade A ~ 2 x 100gm
(shown in Champion 065)

Shade B ~ 2 x 100gm
(shown in Concrete 061)

1 ball of each colour will work
approx. 175cm/69in of scarf.

I made mine approx. 230cm/91in

NEEDLES

1 pair 12mm (US 15) needles.

....

Using A cast on 19 stitches.
Row 1: Using B, knit into front and
back of first stitch, knit to last
2 stitches, knit 2 together.

Row 2: Using B, knit 2, purl 15,
knit 2.

Row 3: Using A, knit into front and
back of first stitch, knit to last
2 stitches, knit 2 together.

Row 4: Using A, knit to end.

These 4 rows set pattern.

Continue in pattern carrying yarn
up the side not in use, until scarf
measures desired length, ending with
row 3.

Using A, cast off knitways.

Voyager Hat

Materials:

YARN USED

Rowan Big Wool
(shown in Blue Velvet 026)

NEEDLES

1 pair 10mm (US 15) needles.

Cast on 41 stitches.

Row 1: Knit 1, * purl 1, knit 1, repeat from * to end.

This row sets moss stitch.

Work in moss stitch until hat measures 10cm/4in, ending with right side facing for next row.

Beginning with a knit row, work in stocking stitch (1 row knit, 1 row purl) until hat measures 17cm/7in, ending with right side facing for next row.

Shape crown
Next row: *(Knit 6, knit 2 stitches together) repeat from * to last stitch. (36 stitches remain)

Next row: Purl.

Next row: *(Knit 5, knit 2 stitches together) repeat from * to last stitch. (31 stitches remain)

Next row: Purl.

Next row: *(Knit 4, knit 2 stitches together) repeat from * to last stitch. (26 stitches remain)

Next row: Purl 1, *(purl 2 together, purl 3) repeat from * to last stitch. (21 stitches remain)

Next row: *(Knit 2, knit 2 stitches together) repeat from * to last stitch, knit 1. (16 stitches remain)

Next row: Purl 1, *(purl 2 stitches together, purl 1) repeat from * to last stitch. (11 stitches remain)

Next row: *(Knit 2 stitches together) repeat from * to last stitch, knit 1. (6 stitches remain)

Break yarn and thread through the remaining stitches. Pull together.

Fasten off.

Using mattress stitch join back seam.

Button trim
Pile up buttons of various sizes and join together using embroidery thread in a contrasting colour then attach to hat.

—— Wanderer Cardigan ——

TO FIT

S	M	L	XL	XXL	
81~86	92~97	101~107	112~117	122~127	cm
32~34	36~38	40~42	44~46	48~50	in

Actual Measurements (laid flat)

Width 45.5 [50.5:56.5:62.5:69.5]cm/
7½ [19½:22:24½:27]in

Length 54 [56:58:60:62]cm/
21½ [22:23:23½:24½]in

Sleeve length 46 [47:48:48:48]cm/
18 [18½:19:19:19]in

YARN USED
Rowan Lima (shown in Argentina 893)
9 [9:10:12:13] x 50gm

YARN AMOUNTS ARE BASED ON AVERAGE REQUIREMENT AND ARE THEREFORE
APPROXIMATE

NEEDLES
1 pair 5½mm (US 9) needles
1 pair 4½mm (US 7) needles

EXTRAS
2 Stitch holders
1 button

TENSION
20 stitches and 26rows to 10cm/4in measured over stocking stitch
on 5½mm (US 9) needles.

BACK
Using 4½mm needles cast on 91 [101:113:125:139] stitches.

Row 1 (Right side): Knit 1, * purl 1, knit 1, repeat from * to end.

Row 2: * Purl 1, knit 1, repeat from * to last stitch, purl 1.

Row 3: Purl 1, * knit 1, purl 1, repeat from * to end.

Row 4: * Knit 1, purl 1, repeat from * to last stitch, knit 1.

These 4 rows set double moss stitch pattern.

Work 4 rows more in patt.

Change to 5½mm needles and continue in pattern as set until work measures 9 [9:10:10:10]cm/3¾ [3¾:4:4:4]in, ending with right side facing for next row.

Beginning with a knit row, continue in stocking stitch (1 row knit, 1 row purl) until work measures 32 [33:34:35:36]cm/ 12½ [13:13½:13¾:14]in, ending with right side facing for next row.

Work 2 rows.

Shape armhole
Decrease 1 stitch at each end of next 6 [6:8:8:10] rows. (79 [89:97:109:119] stitches)

Continue without shaping until armhole measures 19 [20:21:22:23] cm/7½ [8:8¼:8½:9]in, ending with right side facing for next row.

Shape shoulders and back neck
Next row: Knit 22 [27:30:36:40], turn and leave remaining stitches on a holder.

Work each side of neck separately.

Next row: Purl 2 together, purl to end.

Next row: Cast off 9 [12:13:16:18] stitches, knit to last 2 stitches, knit 2 together.

Next row: Purl 2 together, purl to end.

Cast off remaining stitches.

With RS facing, rejoin yarn to rem stitches, cast off centre 35 [35:37:37:39] stitches, knit to end.

Next row: Purl to last 2 stitches, purl 2 together.

Next row: Knit 2 together, knit to end.

Next row: Cast off 9 [12:13:16:18] stitches, knit to last 2 stitches, knit 2 together.

Knit 1 row.

Cast off remaining stitches.

LEFT FRONT
Using 4½mm needles cast on 51 [57:63:69:75] stitches.

Work 8 rows in double moss stitch as set on back.

Change to 5½mm needles and continue in double moss stitch until work measures 9 [9:10:10:10]cm/ 3¾ [3¾:4:4:4]in, ending with right side facing for next row.

Continue as follows:-

Row 1 (right side): Knit to last 9 stitches, work 9 stitches in double moss stitch.

Row 2: Work 9 stitches in double moss stitch, purl to end.

These 2 rows set double moss stitch placement at front edge and stocking stitch on remaining stitches.

Continue as set until work measures 32 [33:34:35:36]cm/ 12½ [13:13½:13¾:14]in, ending with right side facing for next row.

Work 2 rows.

Shape armhole and front neck
Next row: Decrease 1 stitch at beginning of row, knit to last 11 stitches, knit 2 together, work 9 stitches in double moss stitch.

Next row: Work 9 stitches in double moss stitch, purl to last 2 stitches, decrease 1 stitch.

These 2 rows set armhole and front neck shaping.

Decrease 1 stitch at armhole edge of following 4 [4:6:6:8] rows and AT SAME TIME decrease 1 stitch at neck edge of next and 1 [1:2:2:3] following alternate rows. (42 [48:51:57:60] stitches remain)

Decrease 1 stitch at neck edge of next and 8 [9:11:11:11] following alternate rows and then on every following 4th row until 28 [33:36:42:46] stitches remain.

Continue without shaping until armhole measures 19 [20:21:22:23] cm/7½ [8:8¼:8½:9]in, ending with right side facing for next row.

Shape shoulder
Next row: Cast off 9 [12:13:16:18] stitches, pattern to end.

Work 1 row.

Next row: Cast off 10 [12:14:17:19] stitches, pattern to end. (9 stitches)

Leave these 9 stitches on a holder, do not break off yarn.

RIGHT FRONT
Using 4½mm needles cast on 51 [57:63:69:75] stitches.

Work 8 rows in double moss stitch as set on back.

Change to 5½mm needles and continue in double moss stitch until work measures 9 [9:10:10:10]cm/ 3¾ [3¾:4:4:4]in, ending with right side facing for next row.

Continue as follows:-

Row 1 (right side): Work 9 stitches in double moss stitch, knit to end.

Row 2: Purl to last 9 stitches, work 9 stitches in double moss stitch.

These 2 rows set double moss stitch placement at front edge and stocking stitch on remaining stitches.

Continue as set until work measures 32 [33:34:35:36]cm/ 12½ [13:13½:13¾:14]in, ending with right side facing for next row.

Next row (buttonhole row): Pattern 4, work 2 stitches tgoether, yarn forward and over needle, pattern as set to end.

Work 1 row.

Shape armhole and front neck
Next row: Work 9 stitches in double moss stitch, knit 2 together through back of loop, knit to last 2 stitches, decrease 1 stitch.

Next row: Decrease 1 stitch, purl to last 9 stitches, work 9 stitches in double moss stitch.

These 2 rows set armhole and front neck shaping.

Decrease 1 stitch at armhole edge of following 4 [4:6:6:8] rows and AT SAME TIME decrease 1 stitch at neck edge of next and 1 [1:2:2:3:3] following alternate rows. (42 [48:51:57:60] stitches remain)

Decrease 1 stitch at neck edge of next and 8 [9:11:11:11] following alternate rows and then on every following 4th row until 28 [33:36:42:46] stitches remain.

Continue without shaping until armhole measures 19 [20:21:22:23] cm/7½ [8:8¾:8½:9]in, ending with wrong side facing for next row.

Shape shoulder
Next row: Cast off 9 [12:13:16:18] stitches, pattern to end.

Work 1 row.

Next row: Cast off 10 [12:14:17:19] stitches, pattern to end. (9 stitches)

Leave these 9 stitches on a holder, do not break off yarn.

SLEEVES (Both alike)
Using 4½mm needles cast on 45 [45:47:47:49] stitches.

Work 8 rows in double moss stitch as set on back.

Change to 5½mm needles and continue in double moss stitch until work measures 7 [7:8:8:8]cm/ 2¾ [2¾:3:3:3]in, ending with right side facing for next row.

Beginning with a knit row and working in stocking stitch throughout, increase 1 stitch at each end of next and 0 [4:6:13:18] foll 0 [4th:4th:4th:4th] row, then on every foll 6th row to 77 [81:85:89:93] stitches.

Continue until work measures 46 [47:48:48:48]cm/18 [18½:19:19:19] in, ending with right side facing for next row.

Shape sleeve top
Decrease 1 stitch at each end of next 6 [6:8:8:10] rows. (65 [69:69:73:73] stitches remain)

Cast off 9 stitches at beginning of next 6 rows. (11 [15:15:19:19] stitches remain)

Cast off.

MAKING UP
Join both shoulder seams, using mattress stitch.

Button and Front edging

Using 4½mm needles continue in double moss stitch on each set of 9 stitches left on a holder until this band fits around to centre back neck, sewing in position at same time. Join these bands at the back neck.

Join side and sleeve seams, using mattress stitch. Sew sleeves in position. Sew on button.

Venturer Tunic

TO FIT

S	M	L	XL	XXL	
81~86	92~97	101~107	112~117	122~127	cm
32~34	36~38	40~42	44~46	48~50	in

Actual Measurements (laid flat)

Width   49 [53:60:66:73]cm/19½ [21:23½:26:28½]in

Length 74 [75:76:77:78]cm/29 [29½:30:30½:30½]in

Sleeve length:

46 [47:48:48:48]cm/18 [18½:19:19:19]in

YARN USED

Rowan Cocoon (shown in Scree 803)

7 [8:9:9:10] x 100gm

YARN AMOUNTS ARE BASED ON AVERAGE REQUIREMENT AND ARE THEREFORE APPROXIMATE

NEEDLES

1 pair 6mm (US 10) needles
1 pair 7mm (US 10½) needles

EXTRAS

Stitch holders

TENSION

14 stitches and 19 rows to 10cm/4in measured over stocking stitch on 7mm (US 10½) needles.

BACK

Using 6mm needles cast on 70 [74:86:94:102] stitches.

Row 1 (Right side): Knit 2, * purl 2, knit 2, repeat from * to end.

Row 2: * Purl 2, knit 2, repeat from * to last 2 stitches, purl 2.

These 2 rows set rib.

Continue in rib as set until work measures 9 [9:10:10:10]cm/ 3½ [3½:4:4:4]in, ending with wrong side facing for next row.

Next row (wrong side): Working in rib, decrease 1 [0:1:1:0] stitch at each end of row. (68 [74:84:92:102] stitches remain)

Change to 7mm needles and beginning with a knit row, continue in stocking stitch (1 row knit, 1 row purl) until work measures 52cm/20½in, ending with right side facing for next row.

Shape armhole

Decrease 1 stitch at each end of next 6 [6:8:8:10] rows. (56 [62:68:76:82] stitches) **

Continue without shaping until armhole measures 21 [22:23:24:25]cm /8¼ [8½:8¾:9:9¾]in, ending with right side facing for next row.

Shape shoulders and back neck

Cast off 7 [8:9:11:12] stitches at beginning of next 2 rows.

Cast off 7 [9:9:11:13] stitches at beginning of next 2 rows.

Leave remaining 28 [28:32:32:32] stitches on a holder.

FRONT

Work as given for back to **.

Continue without shaping until armhole measures 14 [15:15:16:17cm/ 5½ [6:6:6¼:6½]in, ending with right side facing for next row.

Shape front neck

Next row: Knit 19 [22:25:27:32], turn and leave remaining stitches on a holder.

Working on these stitches only continue as follows:-

Work 1 row.

Decrease 1 stitch as neck edge of next 3 [3:5:1:5] rows, then on 2 [2:2:4:2] following alternate rows. (14 [17:18:22:25] stitches remain)

Continue without shaping until armhole matches back to start of shoulder shaping, ending with right side facing for next row.

Shape shoulder

Next row: Cast off 7 [8:9:11:12] stitches, knit to end.

Work 1 row.

Cast off remaining stitches.

With RS facing, leave centre 18 stitches on a holder, rejoin yarn to remaining 19[22:25:27:32] stitches, knit to end.

Work 1 row.

Decrease 1 stitch as neck edge of next 3 [3:5:1:5] rows, then on 2 [2:2:4:2] following alternate rows. (14 [17:18:22:25] stitches remain)

Continue without shaping until armhole matches back to start of shoulder shaping, ending with wrong side facing for next row.

Next row: Cast off 7 [8:9:11:12] stitches, purl to end.

Work 1 row.

Cast off remaining stitches.

SLEEVES (Both alike)

Using 6mm needles cast on 30 [34:34:38:38] stitches.

Work in rib as set for back until work measures 6 [6:7:7:7]cm/ 2½ [2½:2¾:2¾:2¾]in, ending with right side facing for next row.

Change to 7mm needles.

Beginning with a knit row and working in stocking stitch (1 row knit, 1 row purl) throughout, increase 1 stitch at each end of 3rd and 6 [2:11:5:13] following 4th row, then on every foll 6th row to 58 [60:64:66:70] stitches.

Continue until work measures 46 [47:48:48:48]cm/ 18 [18½:19:19:19]in, ending with right side facing for next row.

Shape sleeve top
Dec 1 st at each end of next 6 [6:8:8:10] rows. (46 [48:48:50:50] stitches remain)

Cast off 6 stitches at beginning of next 6 rows. (10 [12:12:14:14] stitches remain)

Cast off.

MAKING UP

Join right shoulder seam, using mattress stitch.

Collar

With right side facing, using 6mm needles pick up and knit 10 [10:12:12:12] stitches down left side of neck, knit across 18 stitches from holder at front neck, pick up and knit 10 [10:12:12:12] stitches up right side of neck and knit across 28 [28:32:32:32] stitches from holder at back neck. (66 [66:74:74:74] stitches)

Beginning with a knit row, work in stocking stitch until collar measures 7cm/2¾in.

Change to 7mm needles and continue until collar measures 18cm/7in, ending with right side facing for next row.

Work 4 rows in rib as set on back. Cast off in rib.

Pockets (Make 2)

Using 6mm needles cast on 18 stitches.

Work 4 rows in rib as set on back.

Change to 7mm needles and beginning with a knit row, continue in stocking stitch until pocket measures 13cm/5in, ending with right side facing for next row.

Cast off.

MAKING UP

Join left shoulder and neckband seam, reversing the seam for the last half of the collar that will form the turnback so that the seam does not show in wear. Once folded over you may wish to sew the collar in place at each side of neck.

Join side and sleeve seams, using mattress stitch. Sew sleeves in position.

Sew pockets in position to front of garment just above rib as shown in photograph.

My Project Record

Name of project:

Source of pattern:

Yarn used (name/brand/colour/fibre content):

Needle size:

Gauge:

Date started:

Date finished:

Made for:

Comments:

Information

Tension

This is the size of your knitting. Most of the knitting patterns will have a tension quoted. This is how many stitches 10cm/4in in width and how many rows 10cm/4in in length to make a square. If your knitting doesn't match this then your finished garment will not measure the correct size. To obtain the correct measurements for your garment you must achieve the tension.

The tension quoted on a ball band is the manufacturer's average. For the manufacturer and designers to produce designs they have to use a tension for you to be able to obtain the measurements quoted. It's fine not to be the average, but you need to know if you meet the average or not. Then you can make the necessary adjustments to obtain the correct measurements.

How to make a Tension Square

First of all look at the tension details in your pattern. For example it might say "20sts and 28 rows to 10cm/4in measured over stocking stitch using 4mm needles". Make sure you use the correct yarn and needles. Cast on at least 4 extra stitches than the tension states (this will give you the true width of all stitches) and work at least 4 extra rows.

Your knitting might be looser or tighter than the tension required, in which case you just need to alter your needle size. Go up one size if you have an extra stitch or two sizes if you have two extra stitches and the reverse if you have fewer stitches.

Choosing Yarn

Choosing yarn, as one of my friends once described "It is like shopping in an adult's sweetie shop". I think this sums it up very well. All the colours and textures, where do you start? Look for the thickness, how chunky do you want your finished garment? Sometimes it's colour that draws you to a yarn or perhaps you have a pattern that re quires a specific yarn. Check the washing/care instructions before you buy.

Yarn varies in thickness; there are various descriptions such as DK and 4ply these are examples of standard weights. There are a lot of yarns available that are not standard and it helps to read the ball band to see what the recommended needle size is. This will give you an idea of the approximate thickness. It is best to use the yarn recommended in the pattern.

Keep one ball band from each project so that you have a record of what you have used and most importantly how to care for your garment after it has been completed. Always remember to give the ball band with the garment if it is a gift.

The ball band normally provides you with the average tension and recommended needle sizes for the yarn, this may vary from what has been used in the pattern, always go with the pattern as the designer may change needles to obtain a certain look. The ball band also tells you the name of the yarn and what it is made of, the weight and approximate length of the ball of yarn along with the shade and dye lot numbers. This is important as dye lots can vary, you need to buy your yarn with matching dye lots.

YARN AMOUNTS ARE BASED ON AVERAGE REQUIREMENT AND ARE THEREFORE APPROXIMATE

Pressing and Aftercare.

Having spent so long knitting your project it can be a great shame not to look after it properly. Some yarns are suitable for pressing once you have finished to improve the look of the fabric. To find out this information you will need to look on the yarn ball band, where there will be washing and care symbols.
Once you have checked to see if your yarn is suitable to be pressed and the knitting is a smooth texture (stocking stitch for example), pin out and place a damp cloth onto the knitted pieces. Hold the steam iron (at the correct temperature) approximately 10cm/4in away from the fabric and steam. Keep the knitted pieces pinned in place until cool.

As a test it is a good idea to wash your tension square in the way you would expect to wash your garment.

Stockists

AUSTRALIA: Australian Country Spinners, Pty Ltd, Level 7, 409 St. Kilda Road, Melbourne Vic 3004.
Tel: 03 9380 3830
Email: sales@auspinners.com.au

AUSTRIA: Coats Harlander GmbH, Autokaderstrasse 31, A ~1210 Wien. Tel: (01) 27716 - 0

BELGIUM: Coats Benelux, Ring Oost 14A, Ninove, 9400, Belgium Tel: 0346 35 37 00
Email: sales.coatsninove@coats.com

CANADA: Westminster Fibers Inc, 8 Shelter Drive, Greer South Carolina, NH03060 Tel: 800 445-9276
Email: rowan@westminsterfibers.com

CHINA: Coats Shanghai Ltd, No 9 Building , Baosheng Road, Songjiang Industrial Zone, Shanghai.
Tel: (86- 21) 5774 3733 Email: victor.li@coats.com

DENMARK: Coats Danmark A/S, Nannasgade 28, 2200 Kobenhavn N Tel: (45) 35 86 90 50
Fax: (45) 35 82 15 10 Email: info@hpgruppen.dk Web: www.hpgruppen.dk

FINLAND: Coats Opti Oy, Ketjutie 3, 04220 Kerava
Tel: (358) 9 274 871

FRANCE: Coats France / Steiner Frères, SAS 100, avenue du Général de Gaulle, 18 500 Mehun-Sur-Yèvre Tel: (33) 02 48 23 12 30
Web: www.coatscrafts.fr

GERMANY: Coats GmbH, Kaiserstrasse 1, D-79341 Kenzingen Tel: (49) 7644 8020
Web: www.coatsgmbh.de

HOLLAND: Coats Benelux, Ring Oost 14A, Ninove, 9400, Belgium Tel: 0346 35 37 00
Email: sales.coatsninove@coats.com

HONG KONG: Coats Shanghai Ltd, No 8 Building, Export & Processing Garden, Songjiang Industrial Zone, Shanghai. Tel: (86- 21) 5774 3733-326
Email: victor.li@coats.com

ICELAND: Storkurinn, Laugavegi 59, 101 Reykjavik
Tel: (354) 551 8258 Email: storkurinn@simnet.is

ISRAEL: Beit Hasidkit, Sokolov St No2, 44256 Kfar Sava Tel: (972) 97482381

ITALY: Coats Cucirini s.r.l., Via Sarca 223, 20126 Milano Tel: 800 992377
Email: servizio.clienti@coats.com

KOREA: Coats Korea Co Ltd, 5F Eyeon B/D, 935-40 Bangbae- Dong, Seocho-Gu, Seoul Tel: (82) 2 521 6262. Web: www.coatskorea.co.kr

LEBANON: y.knot, Saifi Village, Mkhalissiya Street 162, Beirut
Tel: (961) 1 992211 Email: y.knot@cyberia.net.lb

LUXEMBOURG: Bastel Kiste, Rue Du Fort Elizabeth 17-19, 1463 Luxembourg Tel: 00352 40 05 06

MALTA: John Gregory Ltd, 8 Ta'Xbiex Sea Front, Msida MSD 1512, Malta
Tel: +356 2133 0202, Email: raygreg@onvol.net

NEW ZEALAND: ACS New Zealand, 1 March Place, Belfast, Christchurch. Tel: 64-3-323-6665

NORWAY: Coats Knappehuset AS, Pb 100 Ulset, 5873 Bergen. Tel: (47) 55 53 93 00

SINGAPORE: Golden Dragon Store, 101 Upper Cross Street #02-51, People's Park Centre, Singapore 058357. Tel: (65) 6 5358454
Email: gdscraft@hotmail.com

SOUTH AFRICA: Arthur Bales LTD, 62 4th Avenue, Linden 2195 Tel: (27) 11 888 2401
Email: arthurb@new.co.za

SPAIN: Coats Fabra, Santa Adria 20, 08030 Barcelona Tel: 932908400
Email: atencion.clientes@coats.com

SWEDEN: Coats Expotex AB, Division Craft, JA Wettergrensgatta 7, Vastra Frolunda, 431 30 Goteburg Goteborg Tel: (46) 33 720 79 00

SWITZERLAND: Coats Stroppel AG, CH -5300 Turgi (AG) Tel: (41) 562981220

TAIWAN: Cactus Quality Co Ltd, 7FL-2, No 140, Roosevelt Road, Sec 2,Taipei, Taiwan, R.O.C.
Tel: 886-2-23656527 Email: cqcl@m17.hinet.net

THAILAND: Global Wide Trading, 10 Lad Prao Soi 88, Bangkok 10310. Tel: 00 662 933 9019
Email: global.wide@yahoo.com

U.S.A: Westminster Fibers Inc, 8 Shelter Drive, Greer South Carolina, NH03060.
Tel: 800 445-9276
Email: rowan@westminsterfibers.com

U.K: Rowan, Green Lane Mill, Holmfirth, West Yorkshire, England HD9 2DX.
Tel: +44 (0) 1484 681881 Fax: +44 (0) 1484 687920
Email: mail@knitrowan.com
Web: www.knitrowan.com

Acknowledgements

Many thanks to everyone who made this book possible.
To the wonderful Moy and Chris for such stunning photography
and for being so much fun in the process!

To Juste Juozapaityte, Jenna Hollins and Nadia Altinbas for
making my projects look so great.

Thanks also to the Bivouac for being a great location –
www.thebivouac.co.uk

To Darren for making the book look great and to all my friends
and family for their support.

Kate Buller and all at Rowan for their support. Sharon Brant
for her endless help and support since becoming a freelance
designer – thank you for persuading me to take the jump!